The Ultimate Sacrifice

JP HARAWAY

DEDICATION

This book is dedicated to the men and women who make the ultimate sacrifice every single day. Though we deal with the thankless task of keeping the peace and staring evil in the eye and living with hardships this profession comes with, we do it day in and day out in the hopes that our efforts will someday be appreciated.

I wanted to do something to thank my brothers and sisters in law enforcement to show the world we aren't what we sometimes appear to be on the outside. I wanted to enlighten those who have been deceived by the bad press and one sided videos that there is another side to the story. In the end I want them to ask one simple question. "What would the world be without us?"

My hope is that when this book is done and people see things from a different perspective, that they will walk up and say one thing to my brothers and sisters in law enforcement. "Thank you for your sacrifice."

ACKNOWLEDGMENTS

I want to take a moment to thank my brothers and sisters of Law Enforcement for having my back every single second of every single day out there on the streets.

I want to thank my children for believing in me and standing by me when things got rough for us and I want them to know that I will always love them and be there for them no matter what the distance may be between us.

I want to thank my family for supporting me in the darkest times in my life. I especially want to thank my brother Matt Haraway and his wife Terri for everything they have done for me and continue to do.

I want to thank my friends who helped me hold it together and put back the pieces when I fell apart. I want to especially thank Manny Rucker for the unconditional help and friendship he showed me as a friend, a supervisor and a brother in arms. I want to Thank John Pritchard for being there to listen to me when I needed a friend.

A very special and thank you to Stacey Tucker who has been my inspiration and motivation for finally sitting down and finishing this book. She never let me give up and kept me focused. She pushed me for more when I didn't think I had more

to give. She helped me with every aspect of this
book and I could not have done this without her.
You are a brilliant beautiful and selfless woman and
I love you and am eternally grateful for everything
you do for me.

Lastly I want to thank my mother, Shirley
Jane Haraway who brought me into this world and
raised me with a moral compass that has never
failed me in life. Though God took you from me
too soon in life, I know you have always been there
watching over me and guiding my decisions and I
can only hope I turned out to be the kind of man
you wanted me to be. I miss you every day.

FOREWARD

If you asked any member of today's society what they would consider the phrase "ultimate sacrifice" to mean, I would be willing to bet the reply would be giving your life in the line of duty as a soldier, police officer or fire fighter. That would certainly hold as a truth an each case. No one can deny that the act of putting one's life on the line for another is an act of heroism and selflessness.

If you were to ask a soldier, cop or fire fighter that same question you would get the same answer however, veterans of those fields would probably have a broader view of the term. In those vocations there is an inherent understanding that you could die just doing your job and the possibility is greater of it happening the longer you remain in that profession. It's just simple math. Much like driving a car, the more miles you have on the road, the greater the likelihood of you being involved in a collision. You know the possibility always looms in the background but you do it anyway because you always have.

I have found over years of having been both a soldier and a police officer that the ultimate sacrifice has a much broader and far reaching meaning. My subject here is based on my police career however, as it is the crux of my topic and where I gained this insight. Let me first start by saying that I love what I do. I get a great deal of satisfaction from protecting people and catching bad guys. I despise people who prey on the weak and elderly. While I love what I do, there are days when I think retirement can't possibly come soon enough.

I have been a cop for twenty years now and because I transferred to a different police department and needed to cash out what I had in retirement from the first department to make the move to where I am now, I basically started all over again. This means that even though I have 20 years on the job, I still have fifteen to go before I can retire.

Now no one came recruiting me for this job so I have no one to blame but myself for having chosen it. I watched TV like everyone else back in the days where cops were the good guys and had respect and were basically bad asses that made things right for people who couldn't protect themselves. Like most people that watch TV, I believed it. I mean it was on TV. It had to be true right? Wrong. The fact is, cops aren't all expert marksmen that can hit a moving target with a hand gun across a football field and certainly not when we are being shot at too. Cops aren't all muscle bound aikido experts. Yes folks you heard it here first. We lose fights. We get hurt. We get older and are still tasked with doing the same job the same way we did it when we were twenty one years old. I can tell you first hand here and now, it doesn't work that way.

When I first started this job, I had just gotten out of the army and was in great shape. I had been in the infantry and the infantry believes in physical fitness 5 days a week at a minimum. Running two to five miles a day and lots of pushups and setups tend to keep you fit. Even we small guys come out in better shape than eighty percent of the civilians out there. The thing is no one at the ripe age of twenty one ever thinks about what shape they will be in at forty one or fifty. Oh yes and did I mention your eye sight craps out at about forty? You may spend all your life with 20/20 vision but be prepared to wear reading glasses the day you hit forty. By the way, all the stupid things you did when you were younger will also come back to haunt you because you are going to feel every broken bone, every torn ligament and every strained muscle you ever had constantly once you hit forty.

As I said, the department will not care if you are

twenty one or sixty one. They will expect the same unrealistic performance out of you regardless of your age. They do not have a special place to put you just to keep you around.

Ah yes, and then there are the laws. The good old laws that change every other day and all of them seem to be specifically made to confuse the hell out of you and to make it impossible to do your job. I can almost guarantee you that the ones making these laws have never been victims of a crime and were certainly never cops. Make no mistake, as a cop, you will be scrutinized far more than the scum bag you just arrested for robbing some poor lady because they have rights and I also guarantee you they will not hesitate to let you know they have rights at the first opportunity.

Sound negative so far? Good! That's because I am telling you the truth about the job. I don't sugar coat what I know to be true.

I have no doubt there are some out there that have managed to avoid some of what I am telling you. But real cops know that about 98% of the job is negative. Think I am joking? Think I am exaggerating? Not in the least. I'll prove it. In fact, I'll prove it with one question. Do you think people call the cops when things are going great in their lives? That's what I mean. An average cop spends his day responding to calls by people who have no basic skills to cope with day to day real world issues. So they call the cops to figure out their problems. Property disputes. The neighbor's dog keeps crapping in my yard. I locked my keys in my car. Someone knocked on my front door but I was scared to look and see who was out there. No I didn't get a description. Just heard the knock and called the police.

By the way, did I mention that the police officers are expected to have the answers to all of these problems in five minutes? Problems that some of these people have cultivated over many years? Think about it. If you go to any call where you have more than one person in a dispute of any kind, someone is going to be unhappy with the decision you make. If you give too many tickets, people accuse you of being unfair. If you give too many warnings, your boss thinks you are lazy.

You see being a police officer is a culture all to itself. Cops don't want to hang out with other cops off duty because we want to get away from the job for as long as we can. We don't like hanging out with civilians because we view them as idiots for the most part. Most civilians have opinions about cops that have absolutely no basis other than they saw it on the news or a friend told them. Before you say hey, wait, he just called me an idiot. I submit to you that unless you are a cop or have at least been to the academy, when it comes to knowing anything about a cop, you are in fact an idiot. Don't be offended. I was an idiot too once. Truth is there are many people out there that believe I probably still am an idiot. I still do a thankless job for chicken feed pay for people I don't know who call me their servant and claim to pay my wages though I have yet to see any of their names on my pay check.

Oh and did I mention I have to wear armor to work? What kind of idiot takes a job where he has to wear armor? It takes all kinds I guess. Still think it isn't a negative job? Fair enough. The thing is that is the day in day out aspects of the job. I haven't mentioned the horrific things we see yet because I was trying to spare you a little bit of the ugliness. Since you obviously don't get it yet, I suppose I will expound but only a little because this really isn't the focus. You can't understand the focus without understanding what makes a cop a cop.

Most of you spend your lives in a protective bubble. You read about a murder, or a rape or an abused child and say how terrible. You don't see it firsthand. You don't have to see a child beaten by some crack head parent then listen to the bullshit excuses given by the crack head, the social workers, the system that failed the child. You don't have to use every ounce of restraint to keep from pounding the crap out of some scum bag for what he did to his own helpless kid. You watch TV and hear about an officer being shot by some scum bag that used the judicial system so much that the prosecutors, judges and cops all knew him on a first named basis. You weren't there to hear him screaming on the radio, "OFFICER DOWN! I NEED HELP!" Your heart didn't literally stop when you heard the call for help and you didn't drive 140 MPH to try to get to him to try to save him and catch the scum bag. You didn't get there and see the blood, hear the cop's lungs filling with fluid and screaming where the fuck is that medic unit. You didn't hold his hand and hear him say tell my wife and kids I'm sorry and I love them, knowing that you were going to at some point have to confront them and tell them because you promised him you would. The fact is this job isn't for everyone. It is a personal choice every cop had to make and I guarantee you none of them really knew what they were getting into when they started.

I want to make something perfectly clear to you the reader. Though many parts of this book may sound like an angry rant, it is all based on facts that I have lived through on a very personal level. I felt the need to write the truth based on the real life experience that I have gained. This is not hearsay or conjecture and in my humble opinion, it is indisputable fact. Nothing written here is meant to insult or belittle anyone but to educate and enlighten people from a point of view that rarely gets heard. I do not claim to have an unbiased opinion. I do however back up my words with facts that can be verified and I want my readers to know and understand that I do care how police officers are perceived and want to insure your perception is based on the realities of the real motivations behind what police officers do every day. We are after all, here to protect you.

"SO YA WANNA BE A COP?"

Most people want a good paying job that will put a roof over their head and provide a comfortable life for their families. That's what I wanted. A chance to give my wife and kids a better life. Living in Hawaii was tough. The cost of living was ridiculously high and a vast majority of the houses were old and fairly run down. The truth is we lived fairly poorly and I wanted more for my family.

When I got out of the army, I decided to go to Hawaii because my wife was from there and since she had followed me all over the world in the military, I felt I owed it to her to take her home where she could be with her family and friends. I took any job I could get to make sure we had an income but having no other skills aside from being a combat veteran; all I could get were security jobs. I did fill out an application for Honolulu Police Department however and was hoping they would pick me up. It was a job with retirement and medical benefits for me and my family and an honorable profession that I believed I could excel at. The pay still sucked but it was more than I was making anywhere else and they paid you in the academy. I don't know if it was luck, divine providence or perhaps a curse but I walked out to check on the mail and there was a letter from HPD personnel department and when I opened it, the letter said thank you for your interest and we are pleased to invite you to attend the academy. Of course there were hoops I had to jump through first, such as a psychological and physical evaluation but that was fairly straight forward.

I was absolutely thrilled at the aspect of being a cop. I had an uncle who was a cop in my home town a long time ago and was always in awe of the men and women who wore that badge. I went and showed my wife the letter and it seemed that things were going to get better. I was in good shape and wasn't worried about the physical fitness tests and the rest was just classes, tests and such. At least that's what I thought. Little did I realize that I was about to be submerged into a world of chaos.

Now don't get me wrong, but there are areas in Hawaii that you just do not go into when you are a hundred and twenty pound white man. While a majority of the folks I met over the years were very kind and hospitable to me, there were many that seemed to have a problem with anyone who wasn't native Hawaiian or at least of obvious Island origin whether it was Hawaii or Samoa or Tonga. Perhaps it was just me but it was a serious cultural shock which I had to overcome. It wasn't just the attitudes but the sheer size of these people that left me wondering if I was out of my mind. How was I, a little white guy that weighed maybe one hundred and twenty five pounds with all my gear on and soaking wet, going to be able to subdue an angry three hundred pound Samoan.

That letter of acceptance was quite possibly a death warrant for me and I wasn't even remotely prepared to die yet. I had a family to take care of and I made a promise to my wife that I would do whatever it took to make sure we could survive. The bottom line was this was a step up and I was going to take it even if it killed me.

Ke Kula Maka'i was the name of the Honolulu Police Department's academy. My understanding was that translates to House of Law. It is situated in Waipahu on the island of Oahu. Little did I know that this was also District 3, where I would spend almost my entire career with HPD. The academy was actually modeled after the FBI academy and was a nice facility. The instructors there were absolutely top notch and all had my deepest respect and gratitude. One in particular was a grumpy old dinosaur whose name I won't mention but I'll call him Buzzy as that was his nickname. Buzzy was a senior motorman. This means he drove his own car and was a seasoned veteran. He also happened to be my classes "Tac" Officer. Buzzy was one of those guys you couldn't help but look up to. He always seemed grumpy and was a hard ass but if you paid close enough attention, occasionally you would catch him with a grin on his face and it was usually a mischievous grin like he was up to no good and we were inevitably going to be the brunt of his joke.

Buzzy taught us report writing. He was a master of it and he always explained why he was so damn hard on us if we screwed up report writing. He was ruthless and if you screwed up you regretted it. Buzzy had no issue whatsoever calling you out and making you look like a complete moron to the entire class but I know that he did it for a reason. Firstly, if you screwed up, he made you want to never do it twice and secondly, we all learned from the mistakes of the other. Buzzy was a good man and a fair instructor and I am proud to have been one of his students.

My very first encounter with him was on the second day of the academy. Buzzy walked into the classroom and stood at the front and looked pissed off as was his normal demeanor. Out of nowhere he yells, "Who the fuck has a firefighter sticker on their car out in the recruit parking lot?!" Prior to getting out of the army, I was a member of the Savage Forks volunteer fire department in the town I lived in Louisiana. I stood up at attention and yelled, "Recruit Haraway Sir!" Buzzy stared at me and began ranting about firefighters and asked if my blood was blue or red. Then asked me if I wanted to be a fire fighter, why I didn't join them instead. I stupidly replied, "They weren't hiring Sir!" Suffice it to say I regretted my response almost immediately and spent the vast majority of the rest of the day doing pushups. Buzzy later came up to me and called me a smart ass and slapped me on the back and that was that.

The academy was no joke. There were lateral cops there that had already been through other police academies and HPD did not care. You would attend their full academy if you wanted to be a member of their department. The instruction was sometimes overwhelming. Learning the Hawaii Revised Statutes, which is basically a huge book of laws, was a daunting task. Not only learning the laws but also learning how they applied to police work, what was needed for probable cause and then how to articulate all of this in a report that would get past Buzzy's scrutiny was more difficult than any physical thing we had to do. It's enough to make your head explode.

I don't really want to dwell on my time in the academy except to say that I was extremely proud to have attended the Honolulu's Police academy and over my career there have been times I am so very thankful to the defensive tactics instructors I had there. I am almost certain I owe them my life. We learned from Judo and Gracie Jujitsu instructors and there is no doubt that they gave me the tools to survive what I was soon to learn was a very harsh environment.

THE BIRTH OF A COP AND THE DEATH OF A CIVILIAN

Graduation day was one of the proudest days of my life. A couple days before graduation my senior instructor for my recruit class called me into his office and flat told me that when he first laid eyes on me he was willing to bet there was no way I would make it. Then he said he was proud to have to eat his words. I was on top of the world. Putting on that uniform and getting that HPD badge pinned on was like putting on a superman cape. I felt invincible. Boy was I wrong.

Normally when you start out in HPD you are sent to the Waikiki area to a detail called fourth watch. They would send new cops there to learn basic patrol and the place was littered with cops. It is meant, I think, to ease the new cops into the job and give them some understanding of how things really work on the street. I did not go to fourth watch. I was sent to

15

District 3, into the Field Training Officer program which is basically a new guy riding with a seasoned veteran and he or she evaluates the recruit daily on his or her job performance. Going through FTO in District 3 was the equivalent of being thrown to the wolves. District 3 encompassed Ewa Beach, Waipahu, Pearl City, Pearl Ridge and the Halawa area. What I affectionately call the arm pit of the pacific.

I certainly don't intend to insult the hard working law abiding people living in those areas. There are many people there that are wonderful folks and work hard to stay afloat. Unfortunately I didn't see those people unless they were victims of a crime. District 3 was also well known for being the busiest and most undermanned district on the Island. That's the reason I didn't get to go to fourth watch. They needed bodies and I was fresh meat. I would also note at this point that almost every officer that landed in District 3 put in for a transfer to a different district as soon as they arrived so they didn't stay long.

As a recruit in District 3 FTO program, we were expected to take every single call that came over the radio. It helped you learn, the more calls you handled. The problem is that the radio never stops putting out calls. It was nonstop and you rarely had the opportunity to eat. That didn't help me being as small as I was but I didn't dare complain. I wanted and needed this job and if you piss off an FTO or complain, you can be gone with the stroke of a pen. I had a family to feed so I sucked it up and went hungry a lot.

This time for me was the biggest eye opener of my life. Fighting in the first gulf war was child's play compared to being a cop in District 3. In my first week on FTO I stopped a car for speeding or something fairly minor and just as I got to the driver's window; the car took off almost running over me in the process. It turned out to be a stolen vehicle and the chase was on. The guy drove into a housing project and bailed out of the car before we caught up to him and that was that. We didn't have access to K-9s there like a lot of the mainland departments do so once we lose them, they pretty much stay lost.

I saw more in the first few weeks on FTO there than I have in the twelve years in my current jurisdiction. I can honestly say learning to be a cop there was for all intents and purposes the best and worst thing that could have happened to me. It prepared me for just about anything but also unfortunately exposed me to many things I wish I had never seen. They talk about people having post-traumatic stress disorder like it is something new but unless you are a robot, if you are a cop in any major metropolitan police department; you have PTSD to some degree.

It wasn't all horrible though. I met guys there

that I will remember and love for the rest of my life even though I haven't seen or heard from them in many years. It was a true brotherhood and we took care of each other like our lives depended on it because the reality was, it did. One old timer, I'll just call Ralph, was an older Filipino officer that I had a great deal of respect for. The thing I remember most about Ralph was that he had a wicked since of humor and he wore these damn ankle high boots with a zipper on the side and he never actually zipped them up.

Now there is nothing better than knowing you are a part of something special and something bigger than yourself. Being a recruit, you weren't apart of the district until you had proven yourself. In District 3 that meant not shying away from work and never backing down from a fight. Your beat partners had to know they could trust and depend on you if the shit hit the fan. By my fourth phase in FTO, I had handled a tremendous number of calls and had been in my fair share of arrests. I had to get physical with a few of the suspects. I think the fact that I was most likely the smallest guy in a departments of almost two thousand officers, helped show my partners that I wouldn't back down even if I got my ass handed to me. I didn't give up and I never showed that I was scared shitless the majority of the time. It was more important to jump in head first then berate myself later for being stupid. Once you showed the senior guys they could depend on you to be there and have their backs, you were let into the inner circle so to speak.

I did what I was told and never questioned anything unless it was a procedural thing that I didn't understand. On one particular day, which I will remember to the day I die, there was a call from LC, a senior beat partner to my FTO Andy. LC called Andy and told him to switch frequencies. He asked Andy if I had handled a death report yet. Andy replied no and LC told Andy to bring me up to St. Francis West Emergency room for a death investigation. Of course I heard all of this and my heart jumped into my chest. It had nothing to do with dealing with a dead person. I have seen enough death being a combat veteran but I was more worried about getting this right since I never handled a death investigation. Immediately I started thinking about what information I needed and who I needed to contact and so on. When we pulled into the parking lot I noticed at least five police cars parked in the lot and thought that was strange. Still I was more nervous about the case so I let it go. I noted that Ralph's car was in the lot as well. He drove this huge land yacht that everyone made fun of.

As we walked up to the ER entrance we were met halfway by LC. LC whispered something to Andy and he turned to me and told me to take my magazine out of my firearm. I looked at Andy quizzically as it didn't make sense to me but Andy played it off telling me it was hospital policy that we couldn't take loaded guns into the hospital. I thought that was probably the dumbest thing I had ever heard but since my FTO told me to do It, I complied. The guns we carried had a safety mechanism built in that if the magazine was not in the gun, it would not fire the bullet in the pipe.

As we walked into the main doors of the ER, we were met by a nurse who asked who was handling the case. I told her I was and she told me to come with her to the treatment room, which was basically a side room with several curtained off cubicles. As we entered the room, I saw a body on a gurney that was covered with a white sheet and the feet were sticking out from under the sheets. It even had a toe tag on it which struck me as odd but having never handled this type of thing, I didn't question it.

I saw and noted several things that stood out like a sore thumb to me but when you are a recruit trying to impress literally everyone around you, you don't ask a lot of questions. You just do what you are told. The nurse told me that we need to move the body to an examination room because we were in a treatment room and they needed the room for someone else. That seemed logical to me. She asked me to grab the side of the gurney and help her push it which I did. When the gurney started to move the hand fell out from under the sheet and was hanging down off the gurney and I stepped back as if it were the plague.

The nurse looked at me and shook her head admonishingly and told me to grab it and put it back under the sheet. I felt foolish now that I was being scolded by a cute nurse so I grabbed the hand, which was ice cold by the way, and began to put it back under the sheet when the fucking hand grabbed me back. That's right; it grabbed me and had a grip on my wrist. All accounts of this incident told me that I screamed like a little girl and jerked myself free and immediately grabbed for my sidearm, which as you all know now, was rendered useless unless I intended to bludgeon this corpse to death. I don't even remember my reaction except the sensation of my heart beating out of my chest and suppressing the urge to shit myself and run.

Now I am sure you all are laughing at me right about now and that's fine, but you haven't heard the best part. As I began to regain my composure, it was then that I realized that at least 5 officers and the entire ER staff, to include the nurses and doctors, were all standing in the doorway laughing hysterically at me.

Then to my surprise, the corpse sat up on the gurney and lo and behold it was Ralph. He had taken off his boots and gun belt and soaked his hand in a bucket of ice water especially for the occasion. When I realized I was the brunt of the prank, I too began laughing. It was at that point that Ralph with a huge grin said, "Brah, if you think that's funny, try look behind you." I turned around and was staring right into the lens of a video camera. They evidently filmed the

21

entire incident. I just shook my head and laughed. Ralph smacked me on the shoulder and said "Welcome to B watch brah." That was that. I was officially one of the guys and had been indoctrinated into the toughest district in the Hawaiian Islands.

There's really no single event that I can point to that explains where exactly the civilian side of me was dying away. The fact is part of that was undoubtedly done during my military service. I had taken human life during battle and you justify it in your head that it is war and bad things happen in war. Being a cop though, caused subtle changes in many ways.

You are expected to be strong and not show emotions. The only way you can really do that is to suppress your real feelings and when you do that enough, you begin to do it automatically. Even with things you should get excited about, you don't. That's a big problem when you have a family or even people you just care about because they tell you things that they are excited about and expect you to react to it the way they do and you don't. This translates in their minds as you not caring about what they are doing. Cops all know that this isn't really the case but I have no doubt that's how it must look to a civilian. You also become more cynical the longer you are a cop. Where once we wanted to believe that there was good in everyone is changed into looking for the hidden agenda in everyone. We wait for the other shoe to drop and look for the angle that people are working on us. Being a cop creates a certain amount of paranoia as well. A certain amount of paranoia as a cop is a very good thing. We don't like crowds. We won't sit with our backs to an entrance when we go out to eat at a restaurant. You generally won't even catch us carrying anything in our gun hand because it takes that much longer to draw our weapon if we have to drop something first. People, even cops try to say it's just a job. I can tell you that is a crock of shit. People who work at a McDonalds say I work at McDonalds. People who work at Microsoft say I work for Microsoft. Ask a cop what he does for a living and he doesn't tell you I work as a cop. He says "I am a cop." It defines who we are.

The unfortunate part of this lifestyle is that we tend to be standoffish and keep a lot of anger and frustration pent up. Seeing some of the things we see begins a process that numbs us to a point that the average civilian sees us as the officer not caring and that couldn't be further from the truth. You see, without this emotional wall, we would undoubtedly eventually crack. People forget that we are human and there is no amount of training in the world that can truly prepare you to see the horrific things we see as police officers.

Most of us are idealists. We joined the police department because we believed in right versus wrong. We believe in fighting evil and we did not even consider what profound effect these things would have on our psyche.

One particular case that stands out forever in my mind was being called to Pali Momi Emergency room on an abuse of a child call. When I arrived at the ER, I had no idea that I would leave there angry and heartbroken. There was a weird vibe in the air from the moment I walked through the sliding doors. The nurses seemed subdued and they each had a grave look about them as if something horrible had happened. Each appeared to be trying to deal with something in their own way. Usually there was banter going on but not this day. It was unusually quiet. I walked up to one of the nurses I knew and asked where my victim was and she turned to me with tears brimming in her eyes and pointed. There was a doctor standing near the doorway and as I approached he turned and looked at me and just shook his head. He told me that an aunt brought in her five year old niece and then he began running down the list of injuries this little girl had suffered.

She had several internal injuries and all were about as bad as it gets. She had been found in her bed by her aunt. The aunt told the doctor that the child had been beaten by the mother's boyfriend and then left in bed for several days. My own daughter was about the same age as this little girl and I couldn't even fathom her being hurt like this. But now I had to go in and see the child and I simply was not prepared for what I saw.

I walked in the room and saw this tiny little emaciated girl who had these big beautiful dark brown eyes. The kind that looked like if she smiled it could light up a warehouse. But there was no light in her eyes. Just this helpless glazed over look of resignation.

My heart broke in that instant. This little girl was the victim of being born to the wrong parents. She didn't choose this. She didn't ask for her mother to be a meth addict that was more concerned about losing her meth supplier than she was about her own child. Now I understood the mood in the ER. I walked over to the little girl and reached out and touched her hand and all I could manage to say was I'm sorry.

There I was, a grown man, combat veteran and a seasoned cop and I was standing there looking down on this little girl with tears brimming in my eyes and all I could think of in that moment was that I pray that the suspect fights with me. Please God, oh please let him run, fight, something. That's right folks. I am human after all.

I walked out of the room after a few moments with the little girl and sat down at the nurses' station trying desperately to regain my composure. I wasn't having much luck. I had tears streaming down my face to the point one of the nurses came over and put her arm around me and gave me a little hug. They all could see I wasn't doing so hot with this one.

I finally managed to wipe my eyes, call the detectives and my sector sergeant Kyle. "Sarge, you ain't gonna believe this shit. I saw it with my own eyes and I don't even wanna believe it. "I gave him the run down and when I finished he simply said, "Go get him." When he told me that something inside me immediately jumped for joy and right in the middle of that jump something else inside me said wait a minute moron! I was angrier than I have ever been in my entire life and I realized that I was probably going to do something really stupid if I got my hands on the guy that hurt this little girl. "Kyle I don't think that's a good idea. Can you send someone else to pick this guy up cause I don't think I will be able to control myself." I heard Kyle hesitate as if he were taking in what I had just told him and then he said, "John you got a job to do. Do it and do it the right way. I have faith in you. Go get the guy. You get to speak for that little girl today."

I begrudgingly did what I was told and went to the apartment complex and found the guy and after a short foot pursuit and a brief struggle, I got to arrest the man who had hurt that little girl. There was no celebration. No high fives. No congratulations on a good collar. There was no satisfaction in arresting him because I already knew it wouldn't matter a few months down the road. All I could do was pray for that little girl and hope God gave her a fighting chance at a life away from those people. For once I wanted to see Child Protective Services do their job.

IN THE BLINK OF AN EYE

Throughout my career I have heard so many people second guessing the actions of a police officer. They sit back in front of the evening news and see a snippet of an incident caught on camera from one vantage point and think they know what happened during the incident. The fact is a lot happened before that camera was ever turned on. Did you ever stop to think that something had to initially happen to get the person filming the incident to get the camera out in the first place? That is generally the time when the suspect is doing all the things he was told by the officer not to do. You have to understand that when someone calls 911 and asks for the police, it is because something has gone wrong. Someone is misbehaving to begin with.

Society has gotten so ass backwards that the

average cop doesn't want to even think of being proactive because if he contacts someone he deems as being suspicious, he is accused of profiling or violating someone's civil rights.   Hell these days parents are exacerbating the problems by telling their kids they don't have to listen to a police officer. The other side to that coin is parents calling the cops to come control their eleven year old kid that is throwing a tantrum because dad took away the X-box. Then Mr. Officer shows up and speaks harshly to the kid and the parents who haven't a clue of the fact that a child not only needs but wants discipline in their lives, want to speak to the officer's supervisor and complain. Here is an idea. How about raising your own damn kids and stop wasting your fellow tax payer's dollars and my time with the fact you can't get your kid to obey you.

There's an old adage about police work that's been around way longer than I have. It goes something like "a cops day is five hours of boredom followed by 2 minutes of sheer terror followed by 4 hours of report writing." The truth is those two minutes are more like two seconds. That is generally the amount of time we have to make critical life and death decisions that the rest of the world will have years to dissect and second guess. This is also where we make a decision that will save our own lives or get us killed.

Studies have shown, in just about everything I've ever read, that it isn't an officer's actions that get them killed in a critical situation, it's an officer's failure to act when they should have. The usual reason for an officer's failure to act is that he or she is afraid of how society will view it. So they take more chances than they should. We have gotten so damn inundated with stories or personal experiences of being sued every time we turn around that we start second guessing ourselves.

I've been doing this long enough to remember the days when society let police do their job. Judges threw out frivolous law suits because it was a waste of the courts time. It was obvious that these people were just throwing the proverbial darts at the wall hoping one would stick. Today the courts are allowing everyone to sue everyone else for the most ridiculous things you ever heard of. Who hasn't heard of the ridiculous law suit of the person who spilled a certain fast food chain's coffee on them and then sued because there was no warning on the cup saying the HOT coffee they just asked for was actually freakin' HOT! Really? You needed the cup to tell you it was hot even though that's what you ordered to begin with? The bigger surprise for me is that our communities actually sit in the juries and award the idiot money.

What the hell has happened to this country? We use to be a hard working society that actually worked for what we had and now we are a country of entitled assholes that think we are owed something.

What happened to honor and integrity and justice? Why in God's name are we rewarding people for their own stupidity? And we have the nerve to wonder why our economy sucks.

I named this chapter in the blink of an eye because that is when real police work happens. In my career I've been a part of several incidents that occurred in a blink of the eye which changed an officer's life forever. I think I had about five years under my belt when I first heard the one call no cop wants to hear come over the radio. "Ten fifteen! Shots fired! I'm hit!"

I was working in the Halawa area of the Pearl City district when those very words came from an officer who was working in Ewa Beach. This was back in the days when Ewa Beach and Kapolei were still part of District 3. Now it's bad enough to hear those words but it's even worse when you recognize the voice. Richard, "Rick", had been sent to a suspicious circumstance call of a woman or child crying at a home in Ewa beach. When he arrived, he calmly walked up to the door and knocked. A woman came to the door that was obviously upset and crying and Rick told her why he was there and asked what was going on. The woman said something to the effect of he's gonna kill me. About that time he heard a male voice come from behind the door and say everything's ok Brah and the door began to shut. Rick put his arm out to keep the door from shutting and the male reached around the door with a 45 caliber pistol and fired. The round went through

Rick's arm and lodged in his vest, knocking him backwards. The door closed and the suspect and woman remained in the house. Rick ignored the fact he had just been shot enough to draw his sidearm and cover down on the door and kept his wits enough to not fire when he knew the victim was inside and possibly in the line of fire. Rick tried to use his portable radio to call for help but for whatever reason it didn't work so he had to retreat to his car radio. That's when the radio transmission went out.

Though I was coming from the furthest side of the entire district, I had just taken the on-ramp to the freeway and I floored it all the way to the scene. I arrived just after one other officer. He was getting Rick to an area safe for the medics to come in and get him to the hospital. More and more officers showed up and we went about surrounding the house. We didn't know that after Rick was shot, two more shots rang out inside the house. After a short standoff, we discovered that the suspect had killed the woman who had been his ex-wife and then turned the gun on himself. We entered the house and discovered a child in a crib in an upstairs bedroom. The only good to come of that night was the child was oblivious to the incident and was unharmed. Rick survived the incident but I guarantee you his life changed forever in the blink of an eye.

My own personal experience was somewhat

different but no less harrowing from my standpoint. On television you hear the term routine traffic stop and I can tell you first hand there is nothing routine in the life of a cop. We never know what is going to happen from one moment to the next. Some days are busy and others are laid back. Both of those conditions can change in the blink of an eye.

One of my beat partners, Vernon and I, were tasked to accompany a detective to a home in Waipahu so that he could check the premises for stolen property. It was right at the end of our shift and Vernon and I had doubled up at the station in a single car before heading out to the detail. After we cleared the detail we were cruising back to the station and Vernon was driving. He looked over and saw a Kawasaki Ninja motorcycle parked on the sidewalk in front of a large two story house. It was actually a very nice house for the area. I guess something just didn't sit right with Vernon and he pulled over and decided to run the license plate on the bike. Of course, it's right at the end of our shift and Vernon decided we needed to work longer because the bike was reported stolen. When dispatch told us over the radio the motorcycle was a code ten, I sighed loudly and reached over and punched Vernon in the arm. "Brah, Its fifteen hundred, we should be at the station and you gotta run a plate." Needless to say the fun was only beginning

We got out of the car and began walking across the street toward the bike and from our right a short stocky

Hawaiian guy approached us. He looked like he wanted to tell us something but since we didn't know if he was connected to the bike or just some" lookie-loo", we kept a very close eye on his hands. When he got close enough, he whispered to us, "Officers, if you like the guy on that bike, he goin' out da back window right now." He pointed at the large house and Vernon and I headed for the back of the house.

As we approached the back corner of the house, Vernon was in front of me on a narrow walking path and as he reached the back corner, he stopped abruptly and drew his sidearm and began yelling at someone to drop the gun and get on the ground. I didn't even think I just reacted and drew my own gun. How the hell had this gone from going back to the station to a freaking armed subject situation? I took a step past Vernon and could see a large male with one leg on either side of a window and a rather large hand gun in his hand. He looked up at us and stepped back inside the house.

Now we have gone from just some guy with a gun to a standoff and a possible hostage situation in yet another blink of an eye. Vernon got on his portable radio and advised dispatch of the situation and called for more units. It was a big place and almost impossible for just two officers to contain. Vernon told me to hold the back and he went around to the front of the house to make sure the guy didn't run for it.

Now John Wayne I'm not. I saw the size of that gun and really wasn't looking forward to being shot at especially since I was supposed to be on my way home to my wife and kids. I also didn't like that I had no idea where the bad guy was and since we approached it from one side, I didn't know if there were other exits on the opposite side where he could pop out and get the drop on us. I decided to move closer, yes I said closer to the window that he was trying to come out to get a vantage point on where he might be in the house. I got to the window and gave a quick peek inside and saw the bad guy running around the inside of the house like a chicken with his head cut off. I immediately thought to myself, cornered animals fight harder. This was definitely not going to end well for someone. I yelled for him to drop the gun and he looked over and saw me at the window and ran into another room.

It wasn't long before I began hearing more and more sirens getting closer to our location. I sighed in relief at the knowledge that the cavalry was on its way. A few moments later a guy from the oncoming shift, Roy, showed up and called around the corner to me that he was approaching me. I felt much better now since Roy was with me because he was a former SWAT guy and I knew he could take care of business if the shit hit the fan. When he got to me he asked what we had and I gave him a brief synopsis and told him the guy had a big fuckin' gun. Roy peeked in the window but bad guy wasn't in sight anymore. Roy told me to stay there and cover the window and as he was much senior to me I did what he said right up to the point where much to my surprise and dismay, Roy drew his gun and went through the window into the house. I would give anything to have a recording of that moment because I am almost certain my jaw hit the ground and I had to have blurted out about four paragraphs of expletives. I could hear the guys from the front of the house yelling for the bad guy to drop the gun and get down and it also appeared the guy was not complying. Shortly after that I could hear Roy inside the house yelling and I knew he was in there alone. That didn't work for me and no way was I going to let him face down that guy alone. In through the window I went cussing every step of the way.

Inside the house was a fairly large room that almost looked like a meeting room as it had metal fold up chairs all around the room and there was a couple people in the room which I immediately ordered to the ground as I entered. I could hear Roy off to the rooms on the left and it sounded like he was upstairs. As I entered the next room I was faced with a metal spiral staircase and I could see Roy on the top landing with his gun trained on the bad guy. I ran up the stairs and drew down on the bad guy who was now standing facing us with his hands hidden behind his back. He kept acting as if he were going to pull the gun out from behind his back and yelling for us to shoot him.

The situation went from bad to really bad. Roy and I kept yelling for him to show us his hands, drop the gun which we both believed he had behind his back. At some point he made the mistake of turning toward a door in the hall and tried to open it at which time we saw he no longer had the gun. Almost in synchronization, Roy and I both holstered our own guns and prepared to take the guy down when all of a sudden he turned and rushed us. Roy and I were standing with our backs to about a fifteen foot drop behind us and we both moved towards the guy and the fight was on. I grabbed the guy in a headlock and Roy had him around the midsection and we tried to take him to the ground but that was not happening. I started striking him in the face and Roy was knee striking him in the thigh but this guy wasn't feeling anything.

We later learned he was on a mixture of crystal meth and PCP, both which gives these guys super human strength and they don't feel pain. This also accounts for them being injured worse than normal in confrontations with cops because they don't give up no matter what you do. Now here is where it got really ugly.

People think that just because the suspect doesn't have a gun in his hand that there is no weapon involved. That is absolutely never true when police are in a fight with a bad guy. There is always a weapon there, it just happens to be on the cop's belt. If it stays there that's great. But in this case the bad guy decided he wanted really bad to borrow my gun. I felt him reach around my waist and grab my gun and start yanking for all he was worth. I immediately went into gun retention mode and put my hand on top of his and was pushing down for all I was worth. I was yelling now for Roy to shoot this prick as he was going for my gun but Roy's arms were now tangled up in the bad guy's arms and he couldn't get to his own gun. I decided to give up on trying to hold on to bad guy and my gun and concentrated solely on keeping that gun in my holster. I used a technique I was taught in the academy and managed to break free from the bad guys grip and in the process I went down pretty hard because there was no room to maneuver.

The bad guy decided to lunge back towards me and was met with a boot to his face and quickly followed by a burst of OC spray. I hate using that indoors but I wanted to put an end to this shit and we were running out of options. That managed to stop the bad guy in his tracks momentarily but he decided to make a run down the stairs instead. I was back on my feet and right on his heels. It was at this point that the first of all the other cops on the scene finally figured out how to get into the house.

What we had no way of knowing was that the house was split into two sections and the other officers had been trying to make entry into the wrong side. They heard me yelling that the bad guy was going for my gun and were trying desperately to get to me and Roy. Wendal had made it in finally and was on his way up the stairs while the bad guy and I were running down. Wendal side stepped the guy rushing him and smacked him upside the head. This didn't even slow the guy down. When he reached the bottom floor however he attempted to dive head first through a huge plate glass window and failed miserably. In fact the window broke just enough to scalp the bad guy. He landed less than gracefully with a thud on the stone tiled floor at which time I caught up with him and the fight was on again except now he had a pissed off cop whom he had just attempted to kill as far as I was concerned, kicking the ever loving shit out of him. At some point he decided he'd had enough and a couple of my brothers in blue pulled me off him and went about cuffing and searching him.

Now with all of this going on, what I did not tell you is that when he was going for my gun, I could hear leather tearing. I knew deep down in my soul that if he got my gun, I was going to die. It was in those moments that I literally said goodbye to my wife and kids in my head. It wasn't that I was giving up mind you but I didn't want to die without having at least mentally said I loved them and goodbye To this day, every time I think about that incident, I still get the metallic taste of blood on the back of my tongue and can remember every detail as if it happened 30 seconds ago.

When it was over and the other officers had gotten the fire department EMTs to check out the bad guy and then they escorted him to a car and took him in for booking, I sat in the middle of the floor shaking violently. There is this adrenalin rush that happens. They call it fight or flight mode that everyone experiences in high stress situations. You have all felt it at some point. Like when you look up and realize the car in front of you slowed down abruptly and you slam on brakes narrowly avoiding the collision. You heart beats out of your chest. Fight or flight is similar in that the stress causes your heart to pump faster and the blood rushes out to your extremities. Your hands and legs shake and tingle. Your focus narrows in on primarily the thing that you are facing that caused the adrenalin rush. The world slows down to slow motion and what happened in about sixty seconds in real time took ten minutes for you. Your senses are heightened and blurred at the same time and it can be very disorienting.

Often times, this phenomenon is a prime cause of police officers being called liars on the stand because of how the physiological effects of the fight or flight mode changed their perception of time. For them it did take 20 minutes though in real time it did not. They weren't lying; they were recounting the incident as they perceived it at the time. It is also why the standard for policing is based on what other reasonable officers would have done had they been in the same situation. The chances are that at some point they have been and understand the dynamics of these effects.

While I find it mostly funny now, the day it happened I was terrified and furious at the same time. Roy sat on the bottom stair looking at me in silence for a long time then started apologizing to me over and over. He already knew he had screwed up going through that window and I didn't need to say a word. I just gathered my senses and got up off the floor and walked over and shook his hand and said, "Fuck it Brah. We lived."

BRAVERY VS BRAVADO

There are as many personalities in police work as there are seconds in a day. I can tell you first hand that there are assholes in this profession. Every other day, some civilian acquaintance wants to tell me about their latest asshole cop experience. What I want to do is respond by telling them my civilian asshole experiences but that would be considered unprofessional. I already know they exist. On the other hand, some of the finest human beings I have ever had the privilege of knowing wear a badge.

You see, what most civilians don't comprehend is that 99.9% of the cops out there are good, honest people. We put ourselves in harm's way for complete strangers when most civilians don't even bother calling 911 when they hear the neighbor beating the crap out of his wife. I can't even begin to tell you how many times I have heard the words, "I don't want to get involved." We get a lot of what we call frequent flyers meaning that we respond to certain people's houses on several occasions. One week the person is calling us pigs and wanting to fight with us and the next we go back and he or she is a victim and have to treat them with compassion and respect even though they spit on us last week. We would put ourselves in harm's way to protect that same person who two weeks ago sent in a written complaint to our chief because they didn't like the outcome of our last encounter.

There is a side of police work that civilians don't understand and that is what they call a police officer showing them "attitude." The truth here is that many civilians have never had anyone around them tell them the brutal, honest truth. They are used to people sugar coating what they say and being "politically correct." Cops on the other hand, are usually blunt and don't tend to sugar coat what we say. It isn't that we don't care if we hurt your feelings when we tell you the truth. It's that we get sick of hearing childish excuses coming from what are supposed to be respectable adults.

Making a traffic stop on a speeding vehicle is probably the most common where we get the lies and denials and bull shit excuses from people who are supposed to be grownups. Half of the time these same people have their kids in the car with them. I'd like to offer a little insight on this. If I am running radar and I pull you over for speeding, you were speeding.

Furthermore you were probably doing a minimum of 10 miles over the speed limit. Let me explain this process so that the next time you get pulled over for speeding, you will be educated on everything that happened before hand and you won't feel the urge to insult my intelligence. Firstly we use either radar or laser speed measuring devices. Yes they have been calibrated and were tested by the officer prior to putting them in service and yes there is documentation which no I am not required to show you unless you decide to roll the dice and contest the citation. I also do not have to show you the reading on the device. Why you ask? Because I am trained on the devices and you are not. You wouldn't have a clue of what I was showing you. The courts do not require me to show you the reading. Though there are more things I could say here I will sum it up to this. I don't get a single thing out of giving you a ticket.

I don't get more money and I don't get a day off and I don't get a pat on the back from my supervisor. I am certainly not going to lie about your speed to a judge and lose my job over something I couldn't care less about other than keeping the streets safe. Do yourself a favor and just say thank you officer for looking out for the kids in the neighborhood. Be an adult.

It's isn't about pushing our weight around. It's

about control. Cops have to be in control. Let me say that again. Cops have to be in control. If I show up at your house and tell you to do something, do it. I am not going to violate your rights and I am not doing it because I want to embarrass you or prove how tough I am. I am doing whatever I am doing from one and only one stand point, officer's safety. If I tell you to have a seat on the floor there is a reason for it. The fact is you may be the most law abiding citizen in the world and are up for saint hood but I don't know you. I have one goal with every single call I go to. Control the scene and go home tonight. I don't expect you to understand all the reasons for what we do when we show up. Much of it comes from training. Some of it comes from learning from past mistakes. Whatever the case and whatever it is that we do, it is because at one point or another, a cop has most likely lost his or her life and we learned from it.

Now over the course of years, cops all learn something we call "verbal judo." This is a term we use for the verbal skills we use to gain voluntary compliance in every situation from issuing a ticket to talking a hostage taker into not killing anyone and surrendering peacefully. It is the art of persuasion. There is however a definite need for this skill when everyone around you is a foot taller and outweigh you by 100 pounds. I learned early in my career to use this skill to my advantage because frankly, if I can talk someone out of fighting with me, I always preferred that to a trip to the emergency room. Contrary to belief, I do not like hurting people. I don't want to have to use anything on my belt. If I could get rid of all the crap on my belt I would do it in a heartbeat. The key for my success is simple. I treat everyone the way I would want them to treat my own mother. It isn't out of fear. There is a line you don't ever cross. Cops can tell when you are sizing them up. Treating people with respect even if I was hand cuffing them definitely has saved my life.

One specific occasion I recall was when I was working in the Halawa Valley housing beat. I never quite understood why I ended up with that beat to begin with. There were times I was certain my chain of command was trying to feed me to the wolves. I was five foot eight and one hundred and twenty five pounds with all my gear on. The average person in Halawa was over six feet and in excess of two hundred pounds. It was predominantly a Samoan community. It was a section eight housing area and had many low to no income families. Over the years I had that beat I can say I fell in love with the families I served in that area. There were undesirable folks in the area, as there are in any affluent community.

One day I made a traffic stop on a vehicle for some sort of violation and I ran the driver's license of the driver and discovered that he had a warrant. I arrested the driver for the warrant and was taking him back to the station for processing. He was a pretty big guy even among the Samoan community but he never gave me a single problem. He could have ripped my arm off and beaten me to death with it if the truth be told but he behaved. I decided to make polite small talk with him as we drove into the station. I told him I would process him as fast as I could as long as he behaved himself and would try to give him plenty of time to make bail. At one point he asked me how many phone calls I would let him have and I told him as long as he was using them to try to make bail I would give him as many as I could before I had to transfer him to the Central Receiving Desk at the main police station. I glanced in my rearview mirror and I could see him looking at me and I could tell the wheels in his head were turning. Finally he pointedly asked me, "Uncle, How come you being so cool to me?" I told him that he had been respectful with me and that he got my respect in return. I explained that arresting him wasn't personal and I didn't judge him or think he was a bad person just because he had a warrant. He simply nodded and that was that.

Several weeks had passed since that warrant arrest and I received a call from the housing about several males drinking alcohol at a picnic table near some of the apartments. Now I know most of you are thinking, so what! The point is that it was against the law and I can't pick and choose which laws I enforce. I can however in some cases choose the manner in which I enforce them depending on the situation. As I pulled up I got out of my patrol car, I saw five large Samoan males sitting around the table and each had a bottle of beer. I walked up and was friendly at first and tried to get them to just take the party inside. The problem was I was a cop, a white cop, a little white cop telling several gang members what to do and I was also alone as my back up was on a burglary case. One of them stood up and said matter-of-factly, "What you gonna do about it haole?" Now while the term haole isn't necessarily a derogatory term, this time he may as well have been calling me an asshole. As I said before, cops have to be in control and there are lines you don't cross. If I didn't stand up to them, all of them, they would never have respect for me and would certainly challenge the next cop they came across.

I stood my ground and grabbed my radio and called for a fast back up. Basically this means no matter what call you may be on, you tell the people you are with you will be back and you go to the officer who needs you. I then looked at them; they were at this point standing and walking towards me, starting to surround me. I looked the one who spoke in the eye and told him, "Brah, I got no doubt you guys are probably going to kick my ass but since there's five of you and only one of me right now, I'm going to shoot you first. Then the two thousand cops coming after are going to kick the shit out of all of you." While I didn't yet draw my gun, I did have my hand on it and had every intention of shooting him if he decided I was bluffing. It was then that I heard a screen door open on an apartment just above where we stood. I glanced up thinking oh great, now there's six. Much to my surprise it was the guy I arrested on the warrant previously. He looked down at me then looked at them and yelled, "EH! That fuckin' guy is ok. Leave him alone." With that, all five took their beers and walked past me, each apologizing to me as they walked inside. I had not known it at the time I arrested the guy but it turned out that he was the leader of the gang in the housing. I looked up and said thanks and he said "Nah uncle, you have problems in here you let me know." He showed me the same respect I showed him. I never had another moment's problem out of those guys.

Like anything else, how you deal with certain situations on the job depends on your level of experience. This accounts for the civilian's perception of how their encounters with police officers transpired. Each officer is different and generally the only thing that remains the same is the uniform. When an officer graduates the academy, he or she isn't automatically gifted with street smarts and a sense of how he or she should handle the situations they encounter. Some departments have an FTO (Field Training Officer) program in which the rookie officer rides with a veteran officer. The rookie usually rides and observes the veteran officer and has an opportunity to learn how to handle certain situations and why they were handled that way.

Some jurisdictions do not have an FTO program. The rookie is put through and academy then is placed on the job. This is generally the case for much smaller departments with minimum funding. These officers have a distinct disadvantage and have to figure everything out on the job. I can't even imagine how difficult that is. It's hard enough when you are learning from someone else. When these officers are placed in confrontational situations, they don't have the same advantage of experience, whether their own or someone else's to fall back on. This is where the bravado usually shows its ugly head. This is where the over bearing complaints usually come from. Something I call contempt of cop.

These officers know they have to take control but don't have the tools at their disposal to do it without coming across abrasive. Often times the bravado is produced simply from fear. If I come across like a Marine Corps drill instructor, the other person will be more afraid of me than I am of them. The fact is this is more likely to produce a pissing contest. What these officers have not yet learned is that we have already won the confrontation from the moment we arrived. There is no reason to engage in a pissing contest or argue points of view. To simply put it, you can say what you want but when all is said and done, you will do what I say. I don't need to get loud or speak harshly. I just have to stay on track and not be pulled into such things as contempt of cop.

Bravery in the job has many meanings. Everyone has their own definition of what it means to be brave. I personally think bravery is showing up for work every day knowing it could be your last day. When I raised my hand and took that oath, I meant every word. I pinned that badge on and put on my vest and strapped on that gun belt and I was off to fight the good fight. It did not take very long for me to realize that bravery was an everyday thing. It also didn't take me long to realize why this profession requires brave people to do it. Aside from just dealing with constant negativity, we are in constant danger.

Let me expound a bit here. We spend an average of 8 hours a day driving a car designed to chase down bad guys. Though we have a ton of training in what we call EVOC, Emergency Vehicle Operations Course, we are constantly driving distracted. Far more than a civilian will ever be. We are looking for bad people doing bad things. We are paying attention to and answering the radio. We are trying to navigate and get to places in a hurry. Modern departments now have MDCs, Mobile Data Computers, in the cars so now we are also running license plates, reading the call our partners are sent to so we know if they might need a hand and all of this sometimes on little sleep as we have overtime training and court that we have no choice but to attend. All of this while driving. Yes we are very good at it but when you get right down to it, it is extremely dangerous.

The next danger is when we do stop our car its more than likely on a traffic stop. This is where the majority of all cops killed violently in the line of duty occur. This is also where cops get killed because a civilian doesn't know what to do when those lights come on behind them. I think to have a license, you should know that when the blue lights come on behind you, you are supposed to pull to the RIGHT side of the road and stop. Let me say that one more time. Pull to the right freakin' side of the roadway and stop! Do NOT stop in the middle of the road and don't keep driving thinking I will eventually go around you. If you do that I am eventually not only not going around you but when you do stop I am most likely going to point a gun at you and make you lay on the pavement. The sad truth is more people than not haven't a clue what to do.

The officer not only has to worry about the violator's vehicles position but then after exiting his own car he has to worry about lookie-loos not paying attention to their own driving and running him over or ramming into his car. You have seen the videos of people running off the roadway into cop cars. They get fixated on those blue lights and start to swerve out of their lanes, almost run other cars off the road then overcorrect losing control of their car. That's the sober ones. The drunken ones need no explanation.

While I could go on and on in detail, I think you probably get the picture. Cops do this day in and day out. We know each stop could get us killed. That's part of why you piss us off if you argue with us on the side of the road. I am NOT going to risk my life if you didn't do something wrong in the first place so don't insult my intelligence on the side of the road please. Bravery in my opinion isn't the absence of fear. Bravery in my humble opinion is when you do what needs to be done even in the face of fear. It is my personal opinion that if an officer is not afraid to some degree, he is either in denial or mentally unstable. Either one is dangerous.

JACK OF ALL TRADES, MASTER OF NONE

Have you ever wondered what kind of people call 911? I think at some point, someone believed that 911 and 411 were the same thing. 911 operators take calls from people who probably shouldn't even be allowed to use a telephone. I am not being mean; I am just speaking the truth. People call 911 for cooking instructions. Hello, 911? Can you send the police over here; I'm locked inside my car. Yes, I said inside. Why are you laughing? It happened. Once upon a time police officers had pretty simple jobs. Keep the peace and bring bad guys to jail. The job has changed. Not only am I supposed to be a cop but I am required to be a fire fighter, paramedic, counselor, priest, father to other peoples kids, plumber, geriatric specialist, mental health advocate, ghost hunter, and anything else the public needs at that particular moment in time. I have so much crap jammed in my head in the name of training it's amazing I can remember my own name.

Modern police officers are trained in not just the crime solving areas but in areas most people have no idea relate to police work. We have to attend yearly, at a minimum, first aid and blood borne pathogen classes. Now the first aid classes I don't mind so much however the blood borne pathogen classes are like having your skin peeled off of you slowly. It is painfully redundant. They are usually a four to eight hour class and I could sum the information up in one sentence. If there are bodily fluids and they don't belong to you, don't touch them. We also get training on what they called bias based policing which is another class that actually pisses me off. It deals with what society calls profiling and such.

This is not the 60s and 70s. I couldn't care less what your race, color, creed, gender, religion, age or sexual preference is. The special interest groups out there that complain anytime one of their "protected classes" is contacted by the police are ridiculous and what is more ridiculous is police departments are forcing people to attend classes on how to treat these people. How about we treat everyone the same and stop bowing down and going out of your way to appease these groups. It's the old saying the squeaky wheel gets the grease. If a department can identify and has proof that an officer is using his authority to victimize people of any standing in life, fire the prick.

He gives us all a bad reputation but don't punish me for something I don't get involved with.

I hate when departments blanket policy everything. It is like they don't want to single out the person causing the issue when in fact that is exactly what they should be doing. Single him out and deal with him accordingly. Don't hold widespread lectures, which in my opinion are a waste of time for anyone who has basic moral decency, not to mention it makes it look like your entire department needs the training.

In many cases, a smaller department's officers get better training than major metropolitan departments. In my current department, I have been trained in not only my basic police skills but I am also certified as a marine patrol officer with cross training in advanced marine firefighting. I am certified by the Department of Homeland Security on WMDs and am also certified as a WMD risk assessor. I have also trained as a counter-terrorism officer. I have also been a member of the dive team. These smaller departments have the same needs as larger ones and they either train their own people or they have to depend on other departments for that specialty and that usually isn't free or cheap. I am fortunate in that respect that our city trains its officers and we have the opportunity to do some pretty fun stuff.

With all this training comes more responsibility. More demands on your free time. There are inherent problems with having too much on your plate. You can't find the time to deal with it all without sacrificing your free time. Free time can also translate into family time. This is a double edged sword and very difficult for most cops to balance. I personally made a point of never taking on more work than I had to as far as over time because I wanted to spend my free time with my family. This has been a stake through the hearts of many marriages and I was determined mine wasn't going to be one of them.

So as much training as we get, there's just some things training can't prepare you for. Since I have told you about how negative the job can be, I think it is only fair I add some levity to it so that I don't get accused of just bashing the job. This job has its benefits. You see and hear some seriously funny shit. There have been times when I had to bite my tongue in half to keep from laughing in peoples face. You see some seriously weird things that just make you go "hmmmmm."

One night when I came on duty for grave yard shift, I got told in briefing that there had been a fire at a home not far from the station and the fire department left guys there on fire watch to make sure there were no flare ups. Being the incredibly nice guy that I am, I decided to swing by and take the guys some coffee.

Small towns mean you get to know everyone

pretty well and this place is no exception. When I got there I met with one of the firefighters and gave him a couple cups of coffee and we sat chatting for a bit. While we were talking he was telling me that the fire started in the garage and spread into the house. He then asked me if I wanted to check it out and since he seemed so enthusiastic, I didn't want to say no. I told him yes and he began leading me through the house pointing at various things of importance to fire fighters. We turned the corner to go into what appeared to be a master bedroom that had not been too badly damaged. As we entered, I didn't really pay attention that he was hanging back a little. The room had a walk in closet against the same wall as the entryway so you couldn't see into it upon walking into the room. I scanned the room and took a couple steps more into the room turning toward the closet and there, sitting on top of a chest of drawers was a woman wearing a very skimpy negligee. I shined my flashlight on her and in my startled state I did what all cops do. I grabbed hold of my gun and took a step to the side and shined my flashlight in her face.

It was at that point I realized I was not looking at a woman but the most realistic sex doll I've ever seen, not that's I've seen very many, but the ones I had seen were these ugly blowup things. This on the other hand was made out of some sort of solid material. The firefighter was at this point doubled over laughing at me so hard I thought he was going to have a heart attack. I asked him what he was laughing at and he told me he thought for sure I was going to shoot it and said I made a squeaking noise as if I had just seen a ghost. Now I don't dislike firefighters but I really wanted to beat him to death with this thing because the truth is he scared the crap out of me and it was funny as hell and I was jealous that he got me good.

I think some of the funniest things I have ever seen scared the crap out of me first. The waterfront houses here are enormous mansions. They take forever to check out on alarms. One night while checking on a burglary alarm at a certain home, I was walking around the exterior of the house checking for signs of forced entry. On the water side of the house there was a large kitchen which had huge floor to ceiling windows. It was very dark and my flashlight wasn't fully charged so the light was somewhat dim.

My partner was behind me and as I came around the corner I looked into the house and didn't see anything at first but something just below me caught my eye and as I panned down with my flashlight I was looking at a little kid staring out the window with his hands up on the glass like something out of a horror movie. Needless to say I screamed, "What the fuck!" like a girl and bounded backwards into my partner who was now just as freaked out because he had no idea why I yelled and was trying to get away from the window.

After my heart stopped beating like a jack hammer and I was able to focus on the figure in the window, I realized someone had propped a damn Raggedy Andy doll against the window. Ok, so yes I felt like a fool but the funny part is that about a year or more passed and I responded to the same exact house on an alarm and did the exact same thing when I came around the corner. I had completely forgotten about the doll and once again got the shit scared out of me. Eventually someone is going to shoot that damn thing.

Working for smaller departments where life moves a little slower has been a godsend at times and also a source of great frustration, but every now and then you get one of those calls that just makes you want to laugh and at the same time tell the reporting person they need a hobby.

Of course we have the same crimes as any other department and though not a high crime rate, we stay busy enough. What I found amazing about this call was that the RP, reporting person, gave one of the best suspect descriptions I have ever heard.

One late afternoon in early spring I received a dispatched call. The dispatcher called my call sign and then hesitated as if he were actually afraid or embarrassed to send the call to me. The call went something along the lines of:

Radio: Ida 138

Me: 138 go ahead...

Radio: Area check in the area of SE 40th street and 78th avenue SE (long Pause)

The caller is reporting a rooster in the roadway. The rooster is described as having beautiful red and black plumage and a lovely red crest with a black cone.

(silence) Last seen 5 minutes ago.

Me: ooookay?....138...was the rooster fighting or something?

Radio: (suppressed chuckle) Negative 138. Was just in the roadway.

Me: (Loud sigh) Then it isn't a crime. Clear Ida.

Radio: Sounds good 138...Ida.

Having been completely amazed that anyone would actually call in a freakin' chicken in the roadway, I decided this must have been some very important chicken and decided to drive by the area and check on it. Curiosity had gotten the better of me and besides, I wasn't about to let the opportunity to legally make a joke on the radio pass me by. I drove through the area where the elusive foul was reportedly last seen but alas it had fled the area.

Me: Ida 138

Radio: 138 go ahead.

Me: I decided to check on the chicken and as I cannot find it, I am assuming the chicken did indeed...cross the road.

Radio:

(Keyed Microphone)

(Keyed Microphone)

(Keyed Microphone)

(Suppressed choking cough)

Radio: (Laughing hysterically in the background) Copy Ida....(laughing) 138

My work was now done and my daily attempt to make a dispatcher laugh was more than accomplished as I had gotten at least five chats from different dispatchers telling me they couldn't breathe because they were laughing so hard.

While the chicken all was both weird and humorous, it was only the first of several animal complaints to come in of a strange nature over the next few weeks. We, or should I say I, got several more calls about this elusive chicken but on one particularly warm day, I was dispatched to a call of a cow in distress.

When the call first came in I thought my dispatcher was playing a joke on me as I had told her I was beginning to get a complex because it seemed like I was the only unit being sent to all of these animal calls. I quickly learned that it was a real call. I've worked here over 12 years now and I have never seen a cow on this island. There are some horse stables and we occasionally see deer that make it across the lake and are living in the green belts but no cows. This particular call was odd to say the least as the caller stated there was a cow in the ravine next to his house that had been mooing all day and appeared the be getting weaker as the day wore on. Now I have always considered myself a country boy. I grew up in Virginia and have been hunting all of my life. I know what cows sound like.

I arrived at the scene and located the caller who was an elderly man and figured maybe it was just a hearing issue but he lead me up this incredibly steep driveway and then showed me the direction he had been hearing the cow. I stood there and listened for a few minutes and sure enough I heard it too. It was way off in the distance and the noise was muffled and I have to say that it sounded like what I imagine a cow strangling would sound like.

From this side of the ravine, I could not see anything and knew I was going to have to traverse this ravine to get to it. I started down into the ravine getting shredded up pretty good by black berry bushes and the footing was pretty treacherous. The entire time I was thinking I am going to get down in this gully and run into a pissed off injured bull that is going to stomp a mud hole in me and then stomp it dry. I wasn't looking forward to trying out a Taser made for humans on a 2000 pound animal. When I finally reached the bottom of the ravine I stopped and listened again. I could hear the sounds intermittently but still could not see the source. It was however getting louder and stranger the closer I got to it. I looked up the other side of the ravine and uttered a few expletives and then started up the hillside.

By the time I got to the top of the ravine on the other side, I was pretty tired having had to get through the black berries and wait-a-minute vines that obviously did not want me walking through the area. As I crested the hillside I came out into a separate neighborhood. It was there that I discovered the "cow".

There were contractors building a wooden deck on the back of a house and strange as it might seem, the sound the drill made when it came in contact with the board was evidently that of a cow in distress.

I shook my head and laughed because crying would have just been silly. I turned around and looked back across the ravine, uttered some more expletives and trudged my way back to the caller and explained that sound was not a cow and all was well in the bovine world.   I think this would be a great place to let you all know that if there had been a cow in that ravine, I wouldn't have had the first idea of what to do with it and can just imagine the entire fire department and a swat team and a helicopter with a hoist and me missing out on dinner when there was a huge steak right in front of me.

TAPE ON THE BADGE
BAGPIPES, TEARS AND FEAR

This chapter is dedicated to all of the families that have lost a family member in the line of duty

It amazes me at how naïve society has become. Here in this modern world, with updated news at your fingertips 24 hours a day and still people seem completely clueless to what the world is becoming. On Halloween night 2009, a Seattle police officer was murdered while sitting in his vehicle teaching a student officer. The suspect drove up next to his patrol car and fired several rifle rounds through the window. The student officer was wounded and her FTO was dead. The slain officer was Tim Brenton and he was a cop and a father, husband, son and a brother. He didn't know the man that shot and killed him.

To my knowledge Tim never had any contact with him at all. He was just a target for a bad guy on a mission to kill police officers. The next day we were in briefing and asking the usual questions. Had Tim made a stop on the guy or something? The more answers we got, the less it made sense. The reality of it sank in and the fact was it could have been any one of us who died on Halloween, 2009.

Someone had just targeted and assassinated a police officer. It was a clear case of cold blooded unprovoked murder. The moods throughout that next few weeks were somber and I can bet most of the cops in our area were paranoid as hell. What really boggled my mind was only a couple days after Tim's murder, I was sitting on the side of the road running Radar and some idiot pulls right up beside me. I threw my car in reverse and created distance and got out of my car with my gun out. The guy then, instead of taking the hint, backed up. I yelled for him to stop and show me his hands at which point the light bulb finally went off.

Once I could see his hands I made my way up to him and looked into the vehicle and saw no weapon at which time I holstered my gun and asked him if he was an idiot. I was furious. The guy was apologetic and even told me he had heard about Tim's murder and understood why I was upset. What bothers me is how quickly people forget what happened. Your lives were made safer by this officer and he was killed and you probably were outraged for about the first hour or so until you turned off the news.

Here we are with black electrical tape across our badges. Getting coffee at the local coffee shop and a woman walks up and pokes me in the chest. I look at her initially thinking it was someone I knew trying to get my attention but no, that wasn't the case. The lady noticed a bulge under my uniform shirt and poked it. She just poked a cop like she knew me or something. Then she decided to ask one of the most moronic questions of all time. "Are you wearing a bullet proof vest?" Now here I was thinking she was going to scold me if I had said no, but that also was not the case.

I smiled and politely, even after being poked by this strange lady replied, "Yes ma'am, I never work without it." She then looked at me seriously and said. "Why on earth would you need that here? Nothing ever happens here." I looked past her and saw my partner's mouth drop open as if to say did she really just ask that? I already felt my blood starting to boil and the expletives were pushing through my filter but much to my credit I did not go off on the woman and I simply grabbed my coffee and looked back and said, "Ma'am, I could explain it to you but If I have to explain it, you just wouldn't understand."

November 29, 2009, not even a full month after the murder of Tim Brenton, four police officers with the Lakewood, Washington Police Department were shot and killed by a single gunman in a local coffee shop.

Officers Tina Griswold, Greg Richards, Ronald Owens and Sergeant Mark Renninger were having coffee and working on reports when Maurice Clemmons walked in and started shooting the police officers one by one.

Clemmons was a convicted felon who should not have even been walking the streets the day he walked into that shop and killed my brothers and sisters. Clemmons had been found guilty of crimes by a jury of his peers and the combined sentencing was over 100 years. Had he served that time, these officers would be alive today. Governor Mike Huckabee of Arkansas reduced his sentence. Afterwards Clemmons relocated to Washington State and being a complete waste of carbon, was arrested for assaulting a police officer and was also arrested for rape of a child and some idiot actually gave him bail. If you think the system is frustrating to you, try being a cop or one of the family members of Tina, Mark, Greg and Ron. They have something to complain about.

Fortunately Clemmons next attempt on a cop's life was his last because this time the officer saw him coming and when Clemmons tried to kill him, Officer Benjamin Kelly ended Clemmons and brought a small piece of closure to an embattled police community and their friends and family. Though it won't replace the mother and fathers and children that these officers were, it ended the uncertainty and anxiety we were all feeling.

It's not easy thinking back on the events of 2009. That was the worst year I can remember for line of duty deaths for police officers since I started the job. I have lost friends on the job to the job. 2009 was different. The end of 2009 was especially stressful for those of us who worked in the Pacific North West. I have no doubt it affected more than just us, but we were in the line of fire that year. We worried about the families of those who lost their loved ones and we worried about catching the scum bags who took their lives and we worried if we would lose another officer to them before they got caught and yes, we worried if we would be next.

No cop straps on his gun belt at the beginning of their shift without a certain amount of concern but in 2009, that concern was made painfully real and too close to home to ignore. In some respects I do understand why most civilians live in that protective bubble. If something happens to someone states away, they may read about it or see it on the news, but it's not really something tangible to them. It didn't happen to someone they knew. It didn't really touch their lives and wasn't a threat to their survival. Chances are tomorrow they could wake up safe and sound in the comfort and security of their home and go about their daily lives unscathed.

Even as cops we hear about other officers being

killed across the nation and it does hit home but not as hard as if it is someone we knew, worked or trained with. When the 2009 deaths happened, I don't think I have ever seen the law enforcement community ever come together like I did that year.

When an officer is killed in the line of duty, we honor and mourn the loss with a simple gesture that to me signifies how deep the loss is to all of us. We wear a piece of black tape across our badge. In 2009, Washington State alone had 7 officers killed in the line of duty. 6 of the seven officers were killed by armed suspects. No amount of time and counselling can assuage the pain and loss we feel. The funerals were a testament to the loyalty all law enforcement officers have for one another. If you are brave enough to wear that badge, be it a star or a shield, you are family.

Law enforcement from all over the country showed up for these funerals. What was even more impressive to me was looking up into the rows and rows of seats and seeing a virtual sea of red uniforms. These were the unmistakable dress uniforms of the Royal Canadian Mounted Police. The RCMP came down from Canada to show their respects and unity in our time of need. It was during the memorial service that I heard the most stirring speech since Kenneth Brannagh gave the St Crispin's day speech in Henry V. Lakewood Police Chief Bret Farrar honored each of his fallen officers, as was to be expected, and he did a wonderful job.

At the end of his speech I remember him speaking about those who wished to do harm to the community and the police officers who protect them. He issued a warning and ordered all the officers in attendance to stand and repeat after him. It was at that time he issued his warning and every officer in attendance echoed this warning at the top of our lungs filling the Tacoma Dome with a resounding "SHOW ME YOUR HANDS!"

I had mixed emotions standing there. One of tremendous pride and deep sorrow. Hope for a future where police officers would regain the respect and backing of a community that had just seen that we too can be the victims of senseless acts of violence. The dread of knowing when I walked out that door, that same community that would thank me for my service for a few weeks would inevitably forget these officers.

For my part, I refuse to forget or let anyone I meet forget. When you hear those bagpipes playing Amazing Grace, you cry. It's a given. But what the hell are we crying for exactly? I cry for the loss that can never be replaced. I cry for the families who lost the children they raised, the wife or husband they loved and the children who lost their hero. I cry because I don't know why they had to die. I cry because this so called ultimate sacrifice seems to be in vain when I watch the news and all that seems to get printed or aired is anything that will paint a picture of police brutality or corruption. The knowledge that millions of cops are out there saving lives and protecting your property, your parents and your freedom goes unnoticed and unappreciated.

When will the communities wake up and realize that you have every day humans doing superhuman feats of heroism and show them the support and respect they deserve? Make no mistake. Tina, Mark, Ron and Greg are dead not just because a madman walked into a coffee shop and opened fire but because the legislature and judicial system failed them and every law abiding citizen in this country. This is not my opinion. It is plain unadulterated truth. If that monster had been where he belonged, these heroes would still be alive and protecting you. To those that allowed him to walk back out onto the street, the so called honorable Governor Huckabee and the judges that allowed him bail I say this, I hope you never have another peaceful night's sleep because I guarantee you the families of the slain officer's haven't had one since 2009.

JUST PLAIN COMMON SENSE

There is absolutely nothing that pisses a cop off more than being stereotyped. The public demands that police officers do not profile while everyone constantly profiles us. I absolutely agree that officers should not base an investigation solely on someone's race, color, religion and so on. What the public doesn't realize is that cops don't do that to begin with. Cops work off of the descriptions given to us by you! If you describe a suspect as 3 feet tall and purple, well I'll obviously most likely think you need to seek mental help but I would be looking for a three foot tall purple suspect, if there were such a thing as purple people.

As for proactive patrolling, we may as well stop doing it. Society wants us to keep them safe and catch bad guys and then takes away every tool we used to do that with. Police work is not all "CSI". We don't get to submit every little fiber we find to some mythical crime lab for analysis. Police work is a lot of grunt work based on probability and instinct and knowing the areas we work in. As to not upset anyone here I will use completely innocuous terms lest I be accused of being prejudice by people who don't know the first thing about me.

If I work in an area that predominately people who like to drink water and I see someone walking down the road drinking milk, I am likely to pay more attention to the milk drinker because it stands out. I don't hate milk drinkers mind you. In fact I love milk but I just don't see milk a lot in this area. Now just because I see the milk drinker in the water area doesn't mean I am going to go and bother the milk drinker either. If I see the milk drinker checking out cars or walking in and out of yards looking into windows then yes I am going to go find out what the milk drinker is doing. Why you say? Because that is what you pay me for!

To prevent crimes if I think I see one about to be committed. Since however society is more worried about people's feelings and being politically correct, I basically have to wait until you are a victim of a crime before I can act. Even then I will be called prejudice and I only confronted the subject because he drank milk. Trust me I do not get paid enough to deal with ninety percent of the crap I have to deal with to simply do what you ask of me. Hell, it is so taboo to speak of that I am reduced to talking about milk drinkers. Think about it.

It's ok to stereotype me however because well, I am a public servant. Servant? That term irks me too. I am not your or anyone else's servant. I am a keeper of the peace. I am a protector of life and property. I am not however your servant. Speaking to me as if I am your servant will get you a very blunt wake up call. Go ahead and tell me you pay my salary. That works almost as well. Let me help you understand something here. We are not all alike. No more so than you are like everyone else in your profession. People read in a paper or watch on the news, a story about one bad cop and all the sudden every man and woman wearing the uniform is corrupt. That folks is as absurd as assuming that every priest is a pedophile or that all women are horrible drivers or all dogs hate cats. If you don't know me on a personal level, then you don't know me at all. In fact you know nothing about me. I will say this however as it is almost universally true. We do like donuts and coffee.

You may by now be asking yourself why I am bringing this up to begin with and the answer is simple. Cops are human beings with emotions and though we have them suppressed most of the time, if you push the wrong button you will inevitably find yourself being told what an ass you are. We probably will not say it in those exact words as we are required to be professional. But if you are an ass and you get called on it by a cop that has had enough of your verbal abuse, don't be surprised and don't go crying to his or her supervisor because you brought it on yourself. Here are some very simple rules when dealing with cops that will, I guarantee you, make your experience as pleasant as possible under the circumstances.

1.   When a cop stops you for speeding, stop arguing with the cop. You were speeding and you know it. Deal with the consequences of your actions like an adult. You would not accept the excuses from your own kids that you give cops on a traffic stop so just stop it. Can I give you a break? Yes I can. Will I give you a break? That depends on the circumstances. One thing I guarantee you is that if you argue with me, you will be arguing in court.

2.   Never ever, ever, ever, ever, get out of your car and approach me on a traffic stop. If an officer wants you to exit your vehicle, they will tell you to do so. If you approach me while I am still sitting in my vehicle I AM going to yell at you to get back in your car and stay there. If you continue toward me you are most likely going to see my hand go to my gun or Taser depending on the circumstances. Let me say this one more time. STAY IN YOUR VEHICLE!

3. If I am talking to the driver of a car you happen to be riding in, with all due respect, shut up. I do not care what you have to add to the conversation. If it is relevant the driver can explain it. Whatever you do as a passenger, do not argue with me because you are not the one who has to go to court. Driver, tell your passengers to shut up and keep their hands in a visible place. That's all we expect of them.

4. Keep your hands visible at all times. If I have to tell you that more than one time I will most likely handcuff you. Can I handcuff you? I just said I would didn't I? Yes I can handcuff you for my safety. I am not arresting you by placing handcuffs on you. But seriously, why test the theory. All I want is to go home at the end of my shift like everyone else. I don't want to embarrass you. It really isn't difficult to cooperate with me. I can't promise you a break but I can guarantee you a polite and respectful encounter.

5. This one gets me every time. If you see blue or red lights behind you, pull to the RIGHT freaking side of the road and stop. The officer knows where the safe area is for you to pull over and we may drive for miles behind you after

observing a violation before we turn on our emergency lights.

We are doing several things. We are running your license plates and checking to see if the car is stolen. We are checking to see if the registered owners are wanted. We are checking to see if you have a concealed firearms permit. When you see the lights or hear the siren chirp, pull to the RIGHT side of the roadway and stop. This should be common knowledge but for the life of me I can't figure out how people can get drivers licenses and not know this.

6. Whatever you do, do NOT continue driving just because you don't think you did anything wrong. You will rapidly see the number of cop cars behind you increase and if you continue this, you may even need new tires. When people don't stop folks. It starts a chain reaction. I call over the radio that the vehicle is refusing to yield. Other cops then start heading my way. My adrenaline level goes up because I can't understand why a law abiding citizen isn't stopping for the police vehicle. You are required by law to pull to the RIGHT side of the road and stop. Obey the law and please avoid these un-pleasantries. Remember folks your actions and attitude dictate the tempo of how I

deal with you. You are in charge of how you are treated.

7. Here's another one that really pisses me off. If you see that pretty yellow police tape or a police car blocking the roadway, it means do NOT keep going. It means stop. Do NOT enter the area. It doesn't mean do not enter the area except for you. It doesn't mean you live only three doors down so it is ok for you to go around the car or under the tape. It means stay the hell out! I know you can see the anger and frustration in my typing when I talk about this but this is when people get cops hurt by doing simple and stupid things. My example of this is a quick and simple one but it makes the point.

A huge wind storm came through and since this place is full of pines and green belts, there were tress and lines down literally everywhere. We had a road blocked off with police cars and flares and cones because there were charged electrical lines down that we had not had the chance to get the electric company to turn off. Some guy decides that the cars and flares and cones didn't apply to him and he drove around heading right for the lines. I had to risk my own life to stop him before he fried himself. This happens all the time though. People entering unsecured crime scenes. Not only did they endanger themselves but trampling potential evidence then asking why the cops didn't catch the guy.

8. If you are lost and you see a cop standing next to a car he has obviously pulled over, do NOT pull up behind him or next to him and ask for directions. You aren't going to be more lost if you have to wait another 5 minutes for the officer to conclude his business. Go further down the road and pull over and wait.

9. Do NOT ever lay your hands on a cop. If you do, expect a very negative response. It will not go well for you.

10. If you have a firearm or weapon and an officer asks you if you have a gun or any weapons, do NOT reach for it to show where it is. Simply acknowledge that you have it and tell the officer the location. No I do not want you to go get it. Leave it alone. Mistakes of this sort can get you killed. Don't do it ever!

I could go on and on with dos and don'ts but if I really need to do that, I don't think It would be of much benefit. You see dealing with a police officer only requires you to use common sense and have an understanding that the officer is simply doing his job and it isn't personal. People seem to want to blame officers for the predicament they are in when the fact is it has nothing to do with the officer. We don't make the laws. Hell the truth is we may not even agree with some of them but we don't get to choose them either. You have probably seen videos on your computer of these so called rights activists shoving cameras or cell phones in police officer's faces during contacts. You see the police officers tell them to put down the phone or camera and assume the officer is just concerned with being videotaped or recorded.

What you don't know is that every department gets notified by other departments on new weapons that some idiot out there has devised. You don't know that we know for a fact people have now made 22 caliber pistols that are disguised as cell phones and video cameras. Don't take my word for it either. You can see them for yourself on the same web site you watched the "rogue cop" get angry because some idiot intentionally put an officer in an unknown situation to get that response.

Yes you do absolutely have a right to record a police officer in a public area. I am not asking you to forfeit your rights to do so. I am simply explaining that you only know one part of that story and that is from a person who is absolutely going out of their way to make all police officers look like Nazi thugs. They are claiming that we are trying to take away your rights and freedoms without cause. None of this could be further from the truth. The truth is, a huge majority of police officers were also former military and fought to ensure you never have to worry about losing your freedom. Blaming police officers for enforcing a law you don't agree with is about as intelligent as blaming the cashier at a store because the store doesn't have your favorite brand of peanut butter. They don't have any control what so ever over such things. Nor does a cop have control over what laws legislature passes. The truth is you have more control over that than the officers do. Try voting.

It sickens me to try to look up anything on the internet involving police officers because all you see are the few that make us look like idiots or thugs. They don't bother posting the professional contacts with officers that occur millions of times a day across the world. They don't show you the sacrifice officers make and though that happens far more frequently than the bad contacts, you just don't see them on the internet. That in itself should tell you that those posting are deliberately trying to tarnish the badge as a whole.

I recently saw a video of a couple of knuckle heads walking around the Federal Reserve literally harassing every cop they found there. These are police officers that are hired to guard the institution. Now I admit I have no idea what the hell the Federal Reserve Bank is nor do I really care, but these guys were walking up and standing right next to an officer and using a megaphone to talk to the officer with. These cops were minding their own business and like most people out there, tying to earn a pay check. I am guessing their parents didn't give them enough attention when they were children. You poke a bear enough with a stick and eventually the bear is going to get pissed off at you.

These officers did absolutely nothing but attempt to ignore the attention seekers and by the end of the video I was thinking, "Yeah, that really helped their cause. Whatever that is." To this day I have no idea what their objective was but I can tell you any free thinking person would have been upset by their harassment. Being in a public service role does not mean we have to take being spoken to and treated like second class citizens or worse yet, servants.

I am a human being and I will always treat you with respect and probably treat you far better than you treat me but there is a line I draw when it comes to taking abuse from anyone. I demand respect because I earn respect every single day of my life. What I find funny is that you won't see these same guys acting like that towards a civilian because a civilian with take that megaphone away from them and place it somewhere uncomfortable and then guess what they will do. They will call the cops because someone took their megaphone. That is the very definition of irony.

MAKING A DIFFERENCE

Though most of the time being a police officer is a thankless job, there are a few occasions in a cop's life that will always make them stick their chests out with pride. It isn't because they got a bonus or an award or even a thank you. It was because they did something that actually made a difference in someone's life even if it turned out to be their own.   These occasions are usual rare and far between but most cops do have one or two during their career that they reminisce on at barbeques with their family or old buddies or to some young wide eyed rookie.

   For me I think there have been about four times in my career that I feel like I made that difference. I've been a hunter since I was a kid back in Virginia and come from a long line of hunters. Every male in my family for the most part hunts and the tradition and skills are handed down generation to generation. I didn't know those skills would help me find and arrest a murder suspect and gain me a reputation as a human k-9. I was on the graveyard shift working in Waipahu when one of my beat partners called over the radio that he had located an unresponsive male laying under some steps and a very small strip mall area. I began heading his way when he notified radio the male appeared to be DOA and also appeared to have been stabbed. He requested more units for a perimeter and I arrived to assist wherever I was needed.

I ended up on the north side of the parking lot making sure no one entered the crime scene. While I was standing there however, I noticed something on the ground near my feet and pulled out my flashlight and took a closer look. It was blood. The thing is it didn't appear to be going in the direction of the dead man but away from it. I got down on my hands and knees and discovered another drop further away and then another.

I called my sector sergeant Leaward who came over and said, "Whatchya got John?" I told him I had a blood trail leading away from the body and he asked me how I knew it was leading away. I took a moment to show him the difference and he bought into my theory and asked me did I think I could track it.

This wasn't in the woods where I could see

leaves turned up or tracks in the ground. This was in the middle of an urban neighborhood. Still, I told him if the blood didn't give out, I could do it. Leaward called another guy over to go with me to watch my back and I went about tracking. I noticed the blood drops seemed to have an equal distance between them, giving me the idea that the suspect or whoever was bleeding was cut on the leg and the drops of blood were from the stride of walking. I measured the distance and began a quicker track just by going in the last direction I saw the drops in and maintaining the same stride. At one point I completely lost the blood trail and ended up down on my hands and knees searching desperately for sign. I did manage to find another drop and then another and began following more closely. I ended up tracking this blood trail for close to two city blocks through alleys and apartment complexes which lead where they led right up to the back door entrance to an apartment.

I looked down by the back door and found a pair of "flip flops" sitting on the porch and the right one was filled with blood. I called into dispatch that I had a possible location on the suspect and my partner Billy and I covered the apartment until the troops showed up. I didn't know it at the time, but the one homicide detective that everyone looked at like he was a god, showed up on scene.

Now it was all in his hands and Detective

Napoleon came over and knocked on the door. When it opened we rushed in and found the suspect. He was lying on the floor asleep and had taken a maxi pad and covered the huge gash in his right calf.

Detective Napoleon spoke briefly to Leaward who then told me to cuff the guy. They let me have the arrest. That was huge, but even huger was the fact that Detective Napoleon was impressed with how quickly we located the suspect. From that day on I was known as the human k-9.

It was definitely cool catching a murder suspect. That was, after all, what becoming a cop was all about. There is something more fulfilling however and that is saving a human life. Cops aren't fire fighters and you don't hear a lot about cops saving lives in the news. The truth is cops do that on a daily basis and people are so used to hearing about DUI arrests that they don't consider the fact that the officer making that arrest most likely saved a life by getting the DUI driver off the street.

Sometimes we find ourselves called to not just save a life, but to prevent someone from taking their own. A person intent on committing suicide is extremely unpredictable and many times they don't have the courage to go through with hurting themselves so they devise a plan to get a cop to do it for them. Suicide by cop is far more common than most people think.

It is the suicidal subject call that sets my hair on end because I have no idea where the call will take me or how it will transpire. On one particular night I was patrolling in a neighborhood when such a call came out. The dispatcher said there was a male on the 911 line saying he was going to jump from an overpass onto the freeway below. I heard the call and was less than a block away from the area. I didn't use my lights and sirens because I didn't want to spook him and was hoping to gain the advantage of surprise on him. As I came down the hill from the neighborhood I was in I could clearly see the man standing at the edge of the overpass with his back to me. He was still on the phone with my dispatchers and did not see me approaching.

I parked my car behind some bushes and ducked down to move closer and was hoping my backup would get there quick. As I got closer I could hear part of the conversation and I heard the man tell the dispatcher he was going to jump. He stepped toward the railing and placed one hand on it as he lowered the phone. I decided I couldn't wait and ran up and grabbed him, pulling him back from the edge. Though he didn't fight with me, he was pulling toward the railing and I had to force him to let go. I pulled him down the hill to the side of the roadway and forced him to sit down. The man began sobbing and explaining why he didn't want to live anymore, how his wife had left him and his world was ending. I stood there listening, thinking how Ironic. The one cop on the shift that understood that kind of pain was the guy to pull him away from the edge.

I talked to him for a long time and shared some of my own experience with him to help him see that he could survive it if he chose to do so and didn't just throw in the towel. When I got the man to the hospital psych ward he thanked me for helping him. The truth is, in a way, seeing this man in this state helped me. It made me see how strong I really was. I can only hope he was able to find his own strength and things got better for him. He seemed like a nice guy.

The one time I think I felt the biggest sense of accomplishment wasn't really from saving a man's life. It was helping a family hold it together when the elderly patron of the family, who had Alzheimer's disease, wandered off and had gone missing.

I arrived on the scene and interviewed the wife of the elderly man and spoke with his daughter as well. They were very worried and distraught. I set about getting as many assets as possible in place to help locate the man while reassuring the family that in 99.99 percent of these cases, we find the missing person or they simply showed up at home on their own accord. I called in for search and rescue and tracking dogs and we looked everywhere for the man.

As the night wore on I returned to the residence

several times to update them on our search efforts and to continue to reassure them. The incident started at around 7:00 pm and by midnight I was beginning to wonder if this was going to be the .01 percentile case where we did not find the missing subject alive and well. It was getting cold and concerns about hypothermia were beginning to set in.

I was supposed to be off duty at 11:30 pm but told the family I was not going anywhere until we found the man and saw him safely home. At 3:00 am, my sergeant was about to order me to go home and I was now very concerned that I was going to have to give this family bad news. My dispatcher called me and asked me to switch frequencies and when I did she told me that they may have found my missing person in another city several miles away from ours. My heart skipped a beat. I asked if the subject was alive and she told me that the PD for the other city had been called about an elderly man trying to get into someone's car because he was cold.

Though the city was so far away, I found it hard to believe he was there, but somehow I knew it was him. My dispatcher verified that it was indeed my missing person at which time I told her in a very relieved voice, "Tell them to hold on to him, I am on my way." I drove like a bat out of hell to go get the man and once I had him in my car I couldn't stop smiling. I picked up my phone and called his wife and told her "We found him and I am bringing him home to you."

He was cold but he was fine and oddly enough, he had no idea what all the fuss was about. I will never forget the feeling of relief and pride I had when I was able to see that sweet old man back to his wife and kids.

SACRIFICE

I attended a seminar once, on what they called "surviving the badge." One of the things that stood out like a sore thumb to me in that lecture was when the guy put up a chart showing the difference in the level of alertness between a fire fighter and a cop. Now let me preface this by saying I have a great deal of respect for fire fighters. I've been one and am certified in advanced marine firefighting so I understand the hazards of that job.

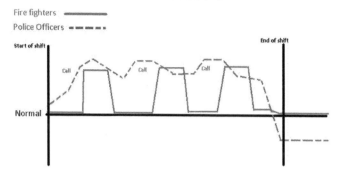

Level of alertness during a shift

The chart was explained that fire fighters respond to calls from the safety of the station. They train and maintain equipment and work out between calls thus they are afforded time to relax in a secure environment. Their alertness jumps up when the bell goes off and a call comes in. They maintain that level of alertness throughout the call and when the call is over they go back down to a normal level of alertness. At the end of their shift, which in most cases is 24 hours, they go home at that level of normal alertness.

Police officers don't return to the station after every call. In fact, their call volume in a standard 8 hour shift and in some cases a 10 or 12 hours shift, is much higher than the call volume of a fire fighter's. They go from call to call never having the ability to decompress from the previous call. Some calls are more dangerous than others but they are constantly at a higher level of alertness throughout the shift because they are always in a position to need to be alert throughout the entirety of a shift. Even during dinner breaks, police officers cannot afford to let their guard down as was evident in the previously mentioned Lakewood shooting.

What this equates to is that when the shift for a police officer has ended and he or she goes home, they don't have the energy to do every day things because it was spent during the shift. If they attempt to maintain that energy it would surely have a severely negative effect on their health even more so than it already does. This accounts for police officers having a lot of issues with their spouses and kids. They still have to go to ball games, dance recitals and make time for their significant others. They have the same every day responsibilities that civilians have. We have the same worries about finances, kids grades, spouses moods and we have to dig down deep to find the energy to deal with our own problems after spending all day dealing with everyone else's problems. These are things that are real and tangible and no one warned us about them.

Adding to the stress in a police officer's life is that we don't get paid nearly enough for the work we do. We scrape by just like everyone else but there is a distinct difference between me getting in financial straits and a civilian getting into financial trouble. You see, as a police officer I have to keep my finances in check or I can actually lose my job. I think it is because if an officer has a lot of debt, the department worries if he may be prone to corruption. I suppose it is all part of that being held to a higher standard. While I do not live above my means, it is still very difficult to live on the pay I make.

Consider how backwards this country is. A cop spends his life serving the community and we pay him peanuts to do that, yet an actor portraying a cop in a movie makes millions of dollars to pretend he is a cop. I don't make much to begin with and if I end up in a situation that costs me my life while trying to protect someone, my life insurance will not even pay for what my house costs. The guy who plays me in the movie will make millions to pretend to do what I did to get a movie made about me. What the hell is that about? We struggle just like the rest of you do and have far more stressors than most.

This is where I really bring the point of all of this together from my own personal experience. I have sacrificed everything I have to be a good man and a good cop. I have spent my entire adult life in a uniform serving my country and the communities I swore to protect. Quite literally, everything I have done since I was eighteen years old has been for others. I was married for twenty years and every penny I made went to providing for my wife and children. I did not go out to bars after work. I went home every single night. My family was everything to me. They were the single driving force in every decision I made.

Five years ago, I had everything I loved and worked for my entire adult life taken away from me. My wife decided for her own reasons that she was no longer interested in being married to me. She dropped the "D" bomb in my lap completely out of the blue. They haven't invented a word for the kind of devastated this left me. I later discovered that in all her spare time she had developed a relationship with a boy half her age on the internet and decided she wanted to run off and be with him. I was so blindly in love with the woman that I was willing to let her go, take the kids and still gave her time to come back to me no questions asked when she realized what she was doing was a huge mistake and destroying our family. I had never cheated, never mistreated her and every single thing I did was for her and my four kids.

My family meant everything to me and I was naïve enough to believe that she would realize that she was throwing something wonderful away and come to her sense. Because of that naivety, I agreed to absolutely everything she wanted in the dissolution papers. I allowed her to take the kids out of state without a fight. That is the single biggest mistake of my life because she moved them so far away I can't afford to go see them much less bring them home to see me. I am pretty sure she did her homework well because not only did she make sure I didn't fight her on any level but she also knew that what she asked me for was evidently not a binding agreement and she could come back later, after she got her way, and change it.

I had always believed that a divorce decree was a binding agreement and that child support set forth in it was also binding. Boy was I wrong. She took my kids and made me buy out her half of the house and moved from Washington State to Florida. She made me promises she didn't keep but then again she promised to love me till death do us part and broke that one too so why should I have believed she would keep the promises of sending me report cards and regular pictures and making sure the kids called on weekends and such. She never kept a single promise. Not one.

This isn't about her and me though. It is about the sacrifices many police officers make that isn't seen or understood. I will never understand why she left. I know she tried to blame me for never wanting to do anything and I don't mind taking some responsibility for that, but not wanting to go grocery shopping? I spent six days a week in a police car for 8 hours per day and my commute to and from work was another 2 hours a day. So in essence, I spent an average of sixty hours a week in a car. She spent almost all of her waking hours sitting in front of a computer. I never complained about it much because as long as she was happy, I was happy.

The hardest part was not losing her. She lost out on a man who would do anything for her. What I lost out on is my relationship with my kids. My older 2 kids I am able to talk to and keep up with their lives and have conversations with. They knew the truth behind the divorce and knew why it happened. My younger two however, are with her and she moved them even further away from me after doubling my child support. It is incredibly hard to maintain a relationship with young children who don't see you every day. These are the same little guys who met me at the door with big hugs when I came home from work. The little guys who sat on my lap playing with my computer. The same little guys who clung to me and sobbed when she tore us apart. And now I barely know what to say to them because I have no reference to see what is going on in their lives. The same questions get the same answers, how is school going, are you doing anything fun? Have you seen the newest movie? I don't know what to say and neither do they. It won't keep me from calling and trying to keep in touch but there is also the fact that I know we are on speaker every time I call. God forbid I have a private conversation with my own children. I miss them.

Did my job cost me my family? I really can't answer that. I don't doubt there were some aspects of being a cop's spouse that are hard to deal with. I don't know how much of that played into her decision to cheat on me. It did however happen and I will someday regain my relationship with my boys that she has now. The fact is that the job does cause break ups in families every day. Some spouses just can't handle not knowing if their husband or wife is going to come home tonight. It is a heavy weight to bear every time your spouse walks out the door.

Cops give and give and society takes and takes. We aren't what the media paints us out to be. We are men and women that feel, love and dream. We have the same day to day responsibilities that you have. We get sick and injured. We do have emotions though we don't let you see them. We grieve for the losses we suffer and still show up when you need us. We are just like you only we are handed a responsibility unlike any other. We do our best with the tools we are given and we put up with the constant criticism that comes from simply trying to survive a thankless job that no one else wants or has the balls to do.

You want my protection but you don't want me to inconvenience you while I am providing that protection. You want me to remember your rights while you trample all over mine. You demand that I show you respect because you supposedly pay my salary and you treat me with disrespect and contempt. You place yourself in harm's way then complain that it takes me too long to save you from your own stupidity.

All of these things cops do day in and day out because it is expected of us. It is high time all of you asked yourself one very important question. What happens when no one wants to be a cop anymore because the pay simply isn't worth the risk to our health, our personal finances or simply our sanity? What happens when the men and women of law enforcement decide they have taken enough abuse and bull shit from the media. What happens when you really need a cop and there aren't any because no one wants to be a police officer anymore? We have all made the ultimate sacrifice. We put others' lives before our own every single day.

Before you say another bad thing about your police officers, ask yourself this. Would you be willing to make the ultimate sacrifice for a complete stranger? The truth is, if society doesn't start supporting police officers and stop making excuses for bad guys, there won't be any more police officers to blame anything on. Who then are you going to turn to when you need someone willing to make the ultimate sacrifice.

THE ULTIMATE SACRIFICE

*"All that is required for evil to prevail is for good men to do nothing."-***Edmund Burke**

Made in the USA
San Bernardino, CA
26 March 2019